HOW TO GET YOUR KIDS TO COOPERATE

(And Help Them Become the BEST Grown-Ups They Can Be)

— A Life Guide —

HOW TO GET YOUR KIDS TO COOPERATE

(And Help Them Become the BEST Grown-Ups They Can Be)

— A Life Guide —

Dr. Suzanne Gelb, PhD, JD

FIRST EDITION

All rights reserved. This book or any portion thereof may not be reproduced or used in any manner whatsoever without the express written permission of the publisher except for the use of brief quotations in a book review.

Copyright © 2019 Dr. Suzanne J. Gelb, PhD, JD

Manufactured in the United States of America.

ISBN-13: 978-1-950764-03-7
ISBN-10: 1-950764-03-6

www.DrSuzanneGelb.com

CONTENTS

Disclaimer   xi

INTRODUCTION

Change Your Parenting, Change Your Child's Behavior.   1

WHAT'S INSIDE
AND HOW TO USE THIS GUIDE.   5

STEP 1

Get It all Out.   6

STEP 2

What's the Problem?   9

STEP 3

What Are the Patterns?   12

STEP 4

Understand Your Past. Understand Your Present.   20

STEP 5

Change Your Patterns. Change Your Future.   36

STEP 6

Make a Plan.   43

STEP 7

Share the Plan and Gain Cooperation.   49

STEP 8

Celebrate Your Success!   56

MORE TIPS, MORE TOOLS

6 Frequently Asked Questions From Moms and Dads About Tricky Parenting Situations, Plus…

Answers, Exercises and Worksheets.   61

WHAT'S NEXT

Resources To Keep Raising the Parenting Bar.   96

ABOUT THE AUTHOR   104

OTHER BOOKS BY THE AUTHOR   105

INDEX   107

DISCLAIMER

This book is a tool that can help you gain your child's cooperation and build his or her confidence.

This book contains educational exercises and tips drawn from my career in the field of emotional wellness with over 30 years of experience. This book is for informational purposes only, and is not intended to diagnose or treat any illness, nor is it a substitute for professional or psychological advice, diagnosis, or treatment. Always consult a qualified health care professional before engaging in any new, self-help resource (such as this one) and with questions you may have about your health and wellbeing.

Any case material that may be alluded to in this book, including in articles, or in interviews [see Resources section] does not constitute guarantees of similar outcomes for the reader. No results can be promised, since everyone's personal development path is unique. Names and details have been changed for privacy.

Links inside this book to external websites are for informational purposes only. Linking does not imply endorsement of or affiliation with that site, its content, or any product or service it may offer.

All link URLs in this book are current at the time of printing. Link URLs may fail at some point if the page has been deleted or moved. The author assumes no responsibility or liability for broken links.

This concludes the disclaimer portion of this book.

Thank you. Enjoy this Guide ... and enjoy your life..

INTRODUCTION

Change Your Parenting, Change Your Child's Behavior

The dilemma:

"My child won't cooperate!"

The reality:

If your child won't cooperate, it's because you've taught them that cooperation is "optional."

The solution:

Becoming a parent that your child will respect and take seriously — by leading your household with firm, loving rules and consistency.

The pay-off:

For you?

— More pride and confidence in your parenting skills.

— Less drama. Fewer tantrums. More peace at home.

— A child who respects your guidance — and actually *wants* to behave well and do what's right.

For your child?

A set of valuable life skills: cooperation, accountability, responsibility, self-esteem and a healthy respect for authority. Skills that will set your child up for a successful, well-adjusted adulthood — and help them become the best grown-up they can be.

Healthy, cooperative kids become happy, confident adults.

And it's up to YOU to give your child the training and skills that they need.

The sooner, the better.

This action-packed workbook is designed to help you navigate one of parenting's biggest challenges, with grace.

Welcome to the Life Guide on How To Get Your Kids To Cooperate

(and Help Them Become the BEST Grown-Ups They Can Be).

Hello and welcome!

If you're reading these words, chances are, you've got an unruly child at home.

You're frustrated, exhausted and tired of nagging and yelling to get your child to listen — and it just isn't working.

And whether your child is a toddler or a teenager, there's something very important that you need to understand:

Your child is not "bad."

Your child is not "broken."

Your child's misbehavior is a signal that something needs to change at home.

And that "something" is you.

As a parent, YOU set the bar. YOU set the tone. YOU establish the right way for your child to behave at home.

Simply put:

If your child won't cooperate, it's because you've taught them that cooperation is "optional."

Children need their parents to be leaders — people they can respect and look up to. This offers them a sense of security, knowing that they're in good hands.

So, starting today, it's time for you to:

Step into a stronger leadership role.

It's time to:

Take an honest look at the problems that are happening in your home, and use each one as an opportunity to **learn how to do better.**

And when you do?

Your child will do better, too.

What's Inside and How To Use This Guide

Inside this Life Guide, you'll find a **series of steps** to help you gain your child's cooperation and build his or her confidence.

Some steps include fill-in-the-blank worksheets.

Other steps contain scripts to help you through much-needed conversations.

Each step is designed to help YOU become the kind of parent that your child will trust and respect.

The Contents page gave you a peek at what's ahead:

Let's begin.

STEP 1

Get It all Out.

Before we can create a plan for positive changes at home, we need to get you into a calm, still place.

Because if you picked up this Life Guide, you're probably losing your cool with your child.

— **Angry** at your child for not listening.

— **Angry** at yourself for not being able to get your child to cooperate.

— Perhaps **angry** at your partner for not supporting your efforts.

That anger might feel like a hot flush across your face, or a cold tightening in your shoulders, back and gut.

You need to **release that anger, safely and appropriately,** before you're ready to move to the next step in this Guide.

Start Here, With an Exercise To Get All Those Angry Feelings Out.

Here's what can you do:

(Read this exercise all the way through, before doing it.) First, you'll need a pillow.

Next, set aside a few moments to sit somewhere that's private.

Hold the pillow up to your face. (The pillow muffles sound. That helps with **privacy**.)

Visualize or imagine the person you're angry at.

Make a sound into the pillow, to **vent** your frustration (e.g., a yell, a groan, a scream).

Say / yell / scream five times to that person (into the pillow, **only**):

I'm so mad at you.

I'm so mad at you.

I'm so mad at you.

I'm so mad at you.

I'm so mad at you.

Lower the pillow to your lap, and take a deep breath in.

Hold your breath in as you count "one, two."

Exhale.

Take a deep breath in.

Hold your breath as you count to two.

Exhale.

Now stand up, and shake out your hands, arms, legs, and feet for a few moments.

STEP 2

What's the Problem?

When parents come into my office and complain about an unruly child at home, I often begin by asking:

What's the problem?

What, exactly, is happening at home that's frustrating you?

From there, they'll often volley into a list of specific "incidents" and scenarios — which is always very helpful.

To find **specific solutions,** we need to begin with **specific scenarios.**

Right now, it's your turn to create a list of specific scenarios — moments where your child was disobeying you, throwing a fit, or being non-cooperative.

Write down exactly what was going on:

One time, my child

_____

_____

_____

when I wanted him or her to

_____

_____

_____

Another time, my child

_____

_____

_____

when I asked him / her to

_____

_____

_____

Another time, my child

_____

_____

_____

even though I'd clearly said that he / she wasn't allowed to

_____

_____

_____

Keep going, until you've written down as many scenarios as you can remember.

Here's more space for you to write (use more paper if you need it):

_____

_____

_____

_____

Now that you've identified a few specific scenarios, let's look for the patterns.

STEP **3**

What Are the Patterns?

Flip back to the previous page, where you wrote down a couple of specific scenarios.

Read each one aloud to yourself.

As you hear yourself saying the words, **do you notice any patterns?**

Maybe one of your patterns is that …

— Your child threw a tantrum and you ended up **threatening or bribing** her.

Then you felt **guilty** for that, and **gave in.**

— When you tried to apply a consequence, your child said:

"You don't love me. If you did, you wouldn't be so mean!"

This made you feel **guilty** and **you gave in.**

— Your child **went behind your back** to:

Get a "second opinion" from your partner — who didn't realize that you'd already set the rules.

— Your child **went behind your back** to:

Get a "second opinion" from your partner — who knew perfectly well that you'd already set the rules, but didn't want to be "the bad guy."

— Your child didn't know the rules, because:

You **never explained them** clearly.

— Your child didn't understand why the rules matter, because:

You **never gave them a good reason** (except, "Because I said so!")

— Your child **didn't take the rules seriously**, because:

He / she knows that you're **not consistent** with implementing consequences for non-compliance. (They can "get away" with it.)

— You really **don't like to say "no,"** and your child knows it, so he / she is easily able to **manipulate you.**

Make a few notes about the patterns you're seeing.

One recurring pattern seems to be ...

_____

_____

_____

A second recurring pattern seems to be ...

_____

_____

_____

Another recurring pattern seems to be ...

_____

_____

_____

Your parenting patterns — whatever they may be — didn't just materialize out of nowhere.

For many parents, they stem from **deep within** — from the lessons that were **imprinted upon you, as a child.**

Understanding your patterns — a deeper look.

Your own parents raised you in a certain style.

You will invariably carry this into your parenting style in one of two ways:

1. Repetition

Typically, you will **repeat** what your parents did:

- If there was yelling at home, you probably yell also.

- If your parents were attentive and read to you at bedtime, you probably do the same with your children.

2. Departure

Another common response is to **behave very differently** from how you were raised — to make a total departure.

- Someone who was raised in a yelling household, for example, may now be a very accommodating, lenient parent, even to the point of spoiling his or her children.

It's essential to reflect on your childhood to make sure that your parenting style represents your current values, rather than being a *reaction* to your past experiences.

Next:

We'll go **deeper** into your own childhood and explore how your past experiences shaped your present-day parenting style.

To do that, we'll dive into a few real-life stories and examples.

The Reason for the Rules: Charlie's Mother's Story

Six year old Charlie asked his mother:

"Why do I have to take out the garbage?"

She yelled:

"Because I said so!"

Then she punished Charlie for questioning her.

This is the exact type of overly strict parenting that Charlie's mother experienced when she was a child.

The problem with her authoritarian style of parenting is that it wasn't teaching Charlie to make positive choices.

The only reason he obeyed was to **avoid punishment.** When no one was watching, he would rebel and misbehave.

When Charlie's mom came to see me because of his behavioral problems, we discussed how her parenting style was replicating what she had experienced as a child.

She realized that she needed to change her parenting style — from overly strict (like her parents' approach) to more positive — a style that would be based on positive discipline.

With that in place, the next time Charlie asked her a "Why do I have to …" question, she took a deep breath, and patiently explained.

Not surprisingly, Charlie began cooperating.

When Children Are Given a Reason as to Why They Need To Do Something — a Reason That Makes Sense to Them — They're Far More Likely To Cooperate.

Identifying one's parenting patterns can take time — and sometimes professional input might be appropriate, particularly if we're not aware our own unconscious patterns.

If you decide that you'd like to work with a professional, it's wise to follow through and take that step.

Your child is counting on you.

But for now ...

Pay attention to instances when you experience something that triggers an exaggerated emotional response.

Like:

"Whoa! I'm SO mad / sad / anxious / frustrated, even though this isn't a huge deal."

Those moments are clues, pointing to possible unresolved emotions and unhelpful patterns. Notice them.

Jot them down in a journal.

In time, the patterns are likely to become clearer.

Next?

We'll explore **how to change those unhelpful patterns**, once you've identified them.

STEP **4**

Understand Your Past.
Understand Your Present.

The following seven stories are completely true — names and specific details have been changed, of course, but the challenges (and solutions) are all very real.

As you read, jot down any stories that remind you of your own family — both the family you grew up in, and the family you're building now.

Understanding your past experiences can help you better understand your present challenges.

Story #1: From saying anything to gain cooperation to giving appropriate instructions.

Jay, father to 8 year old Steve, remembers that when he was growing up, his mother would say anything to gain his cooperation:

"If you pick up your toys, I'll take you out for ice cream."

The problem was that his mom forgot that she had a dinner to go to, and wouldn't have time to take him out.

Now Jay does the same thing to Steve.

Jay doesn't mean to make a false promise to Steve, but he's so tired of telling Steve to pick up his toys, that he'll say anything to get his son to cooperate, often without thinking it through.

Steve can tell when his dad's trying to trick him into compliance.

Because of that, he doesn't trust his dad.

Children need to be able to count on their parents, but that's not possible when manipulation is present.

Jay needs to change his parenting style - from saying anything to gain cooperation (that's how he was raised) to giving Steve appropriate instructions.

Steve should be taught that **if he doesn't follow instructions, a consequence will follow.**

Example:

Jay could say, firmly, but lovingly:

"Steve you must pick up your toys. If you don't, then you can't play with your video game for one day."

By speaking **authoritatively**, but **not meanly,** Jay would also be teaching his son that if he doesn't get what he wants, it doesn't mean that he is not loved.

Love is not only about warm fuzzies — it includes positive discipline — firm, fair, consistent guidance, applied with love.

In this context, children learn to cooperate, and in doing so, they **feel good about themselves**.

Story #2: From threats and bribes to teaching responsibility.

Ava, 7, tantrums when she doesn't get her way — like when her mom (Joanie) won't read her a bedtime story if she didn't brush her teeth.

Ava's tantrums make Joanie so mad that she:

a) Threatens Ava:

'If you don't brush your teeth now, I'll never read you a story again!"

Or,

b) Joanie bribes her daughter:

"I'll read you two stories if you brush your teeth now."

This is how Joanie's mom used to treat her when she would tantrum as a child.

Then Joanie feels bad about threatening or bribing Ava, so she gives in and let's Ava have a her way.

Worse yet, Ava thinks to herself:

"Mom's yelling can't hurt me. If I tantrum long enough, she'll give in."

Ava has learned to **manipulate** her mother by frustrating her until she concedes.

This is what Joanie used to do to her mom, when she was growing up.

This cycle is destructive — frustrated Joanie manipulates her daughter so she'll cooperate, while Ava tries to get her way by manipulating her mom.

Children who are manipulated tend to mistrust their parents — they know they're being conned.

They also think that the only way to get what they want is to manipulate.

These kids miss opportunities to develop self-worth, a sense that,

"I deserve to ask for what I want, and it's alright if I don't get it because I'm loved anyway."

Children who manipulate are at risk for continuing to do this as adults. They've learned that manipulation gets them what they want.

If Ava isn't cooperating, Joanie must try not to let her own frustrations mount.

If she does, then threats, bribes and shouting could escalate, and manipulative relating may ruin family relations.

Instead, Joanie needs to hold a **family meeting** where she explains to Ava the rules she must follow.

Joanie also needs to identify what the **consequences** will be for non-compliance — then she won't have to nag to get things done.

"If you don't brush your teeth on time, there will be no bedtime story that night. And if you tantrum about your consequence, you cannot watch your favorite TV show tomorrow / the next night."

The hope is that Ava will **never** have to experience a consequence.

Why?

Because the intent of a consequence is that it be a **deterrent**, to prompt children to **behave properly to avoid the consequence.**

Ultimately, we want children to behave properly because it's the right thing to do.

In the interim, consequences serve as a helpful tool to support children in behaving properly.

The consequence should be in **proportion** to the violation.

This means:

— **Not too harsh**

Otherwise the child will end up resenting the parents, and may rebel;

— **Not too lenient**

Otherwise there will be no incentive for the child to comply.

Why not?

Because the child may think something like:

"Oh, all I have to do is put a penny in the jar if I don't brush my teeth on time - no big deal."

Ava's brother Adam, 10, also needs to attend the meeting.

Why?

One example:

When Joanie sees Adam, watching TV, she yells for the fourth time:

"Adam, hurry up and set the table for dinner. You know that's your responsibility!"

Nagging invariably causes conflict and reflects poor planning.

Rather than nag, Joanie could discuss his responsibilities at a family meeting:

"From now on, you need to set the table at 6:30pm. If you don't, there'll be no TV for a day."

This way, children can learn to be **responsible and organized**.

Story #3: From not wanting to say "No" to teaching that "No" doesn't mean I don't love you.

When Ruth was a child, she heard the word, "No" a lot. She didn't like her parents because of that.

Now, in contrast to how she was parented, when Ruth's 7-year-old, wants to stay up past his bedtime, Ruth is afraid that if she says 'No,' she'll hurt his feelings or make him mad, and he won't like her.

So Ruth tries to get him to change his mind:

"You don't really want to stay up late, do you? Everyone's going to sleep early."

Many parents resist saying "No" to their children.

Instead, like Ruth, they fend up resorting to **manipulations**.

Example:

They may try to entice, or talk their child out of doing something.

These parents, including Ruth, need to **prioritize being a parent** to their child, rather than their child's friend.

Ruth needs to teach her son that **"No" doesn't mean, "I don't love you."**

Instead, "No" means:

"I'm responsible for guiding you, and it's ok if you don't like my rules, but you need to follow them."

When parents raise their children with positive discipline and teach by example, they're likely to gain their cooperation.

Then defiance will be a non-issue.

Story #4: From "If you don't, then..." to teaching children to do the right thing.

Tommy's mom and dad are frustrated because their 9-year-old, won't cooperate.

Nothing works... even though his mom threatens (just like her mom threatened her):

"If you don't make your bed, you can't play with your cousin!"

And his dad tries to entice him by saying things like:

"If you tidy your room, you can watch TV."

Children who are enticed or threatened, lack motivation to do things properly.

Often, their goal is:

"How can I get out of doing this?"

or,

"How little can I do and get what I want?"

Tommy **only** makes his bed **if...**

— His mom threatens him.

He **only** tidies his room **if:**

— His dad is watching.

Instead of trying to manipulate Tommy into cooperating, his parents should **lay out the rules** that he needs to follow and teach him to **take pride in behaving properly**.

Then Tommy would feel good about cooperating, and his **confidence would grow**, as he thinks:

"I'm behaving because I've learned that it's the right thing to do, and, I like pleasing my Mom and Dad."

Story #5: From harsh communication to patient parenting

Four-year-old Jen asks:

"Why must I stay home with the babysitter when you go to your meeting?"

Her mother, Bessie, snaps back:

"Because I said so!"

This is exactly how Bessie's mother spoke to her when she was growing up.

When you tell your children to do something, it's important to patiently respond to their questions.

Otherwise, they're not likely to cooperate.

Jen's mother didn't answer her question adequately, so Jen will probably be frustrated and may rebel.

Jen's mother could have explained:

"I can't look after you while I'm at my meeting, that's why we have a sitter."

Explanations that are shared with patience and understanding can foster cooperation.

Story #6 From yelling, screaming, and disorganization to teaching teamwork.

Nancy yells at her son, Nathan, who is 11:

"Hurry up! How many times have I told you to pack your backpack at night so you're not scrambling in the morning?

I'm late already - don't make me even later!"

Nancy's household is similar to the one that she grew up in — it is really disorganized and hectic.

Nancy needs to follow an **organized schedule** and she should teach her son to do the same.

Children who are organized enjoy being helpful.

If Nathan were organized, he would have time in the morning to hug his parents and ask if he could help with anything.

Example:

Say Nathan's mother was running late because of an unexpected e-mail she needed to answer. Nathan could ask,

"What sweater are you going to wear? I'll get it for you."

This type of teamwork fosters **respect and responsibility**.

It also replaces the **loud yelling and shouting** that fills so many disorganized households.

Story #7 From intimidation to teaching cooperation

Thirteen-year-old Melissa is a typical teen. She takes forever in the shower.

"Melissa, you make us late every morning because you take so long to shower!" yells her dad.

"I'm tired of waiting for you in the car. Next time I'll leave without you!"

Mornings in Melissa's home are chaotic and frenzied. This is because of her dad's manipulative words and yelling (which is what mornings were like in his house when he was a boy).

This negativity doesn't achieve anything, and makes Melissa feel bad.

Here's what needs to happen:

At their family meeting, Melissa's dad could patiently explain,

"You run out of time in the morning, so I'd like you to shower earlier, or the night before.

Then you won't hold up our family by being late."

This type of communication fosters cooperation and supports a well-functioning household.

Now, let's apply these stories to your life.

Using the blank spaces below (or on a separate sheet of paper), **write down some notes about the stories that resonated with you most.**

Story # ___ *reminded me of when I was a child, and my parents ...*

_____

_____

_____

_____

Story # ___ *reminded me of a time more recently, when my child ...*

_____

_____

_____

_____

*In reading these stories and thinking about my own upbringing, I've realized that some of my **helpful** parenting patterns are ...*

_____

_____

_____

*On the other hand, some of my **unhelpful** parenting patterns are ...*

STEP **5**

Change Your Patterns. Change Your Future.

Your parents did the best they could, raising you.

That doesn't mean they were able to give you everything you needed, all the time.

The good news is, you can "re-parent" yourself at any age — addressing the needs that went unmet, as a child, and healing the parts of you that, for whatever reason, your parents were unable to comfort and soothe.

Think of it as picking up where your parents left off, and helping yourself grow into an even more confident adult.

In this way, you can honor the **best** of what your childhood offered you (all the positive qualities that you possess, today), while also changing some of the childhood patterns that are **negatively** affecting your ability to parent effectively.

In a moment, we'll start to map out a plan that will allow you to **change the patterns you no longer want, while keeping the ones that you do.**

But right now, take a moment to envision the kind of home you'd like to have in the future — and the way you'd like to feel, in that home.

Fill in the blanks, for each of the following statements.

As you do, you'll be making a powerful, written commitment to yourself:

To re-parent yourself and change unhelpful patterns, so that you can give YOUR child the BEST chance at becoming a confident, well-adjusted adult.

Even though my parents

_____

_____

_____

I can do better. I can

_____

Even though when I was growing up, I felt

I can do better. I can

Even though in the past, I have

I can do better. I can

Even though I haven't always enforced

_____

_____

_____

in the future, I can make sure that

_____

_____

_____

Even though in the past, I've allowed my child to

_____

_____

_____

in the future, I can enforce consequences to make sure that

_____

_____

As a parent, I want to feel confident in my ability to

_____

_____

_____

I want my home to be a place where rules are

_____

and consequences are

_____

After he or she has grown up, I want my child to remember our home as a place where

_____

_____

_____

When I'm gone, I want my child to remember me as someone who

_____

_____

_____

Ultimately, I want my child to remember his / her childhood as a time of

_____

_____

_____

Ultimately, I want my child to grow up to become a

_____ adult.

Take a look at all of those positive, beautiful statements — each one, **a new commitment** with yourself.

Know that it's ALL possible.

You can:

- **Get your child to cooperate.**

You can:

- **Secure their trust and respect.**

You can:

- **Create the kind of environment you want in your home.**

You're already moving closer and closer, just by doing this work.

And next?

We're going to **create a plan** to bring you even closer.

STEP **6**

Make a Plan

Now that you've identified your specific parenting challenges, explored your patterns, and outlined the exact kind of environment you want to create in your home, it's time to make a plan!

Your plan will include:

— **Reasonable rules** with **appropriate consequences**.

This means...

Both parents need to decide on best-suited rules and consequences.

— **Consistent enforcement** of consequences

This means...

Both parents need to be on the same page.

— A **family meeting** to explain and implement the plan

This means:

Follow-up family meetings will most likely be necessary to discuss progress and make adjustments.

— Modeling the behavior you want to see from your kids

This means:

"Do as I say, but not as I do" just won't cut it anymore.

— Quality family time on a regular basis

This means:

Family dinners, for example, with all electronic media turned off.

A few words on "consequences."

Many parents struggle to set appropriate consequences and enforce them **consistently**.

They feel **"mean"** doing it.

Like a **"bad guy."**

But you don't need to view consequences as a "bad" thing.

Quite the opposite.

By enforcing consequences consistently, you'll be teaching your child valuable life lessons.

These lessons are a gift.

If you're still feeling uncertain (or perhaps a little uneasy) about why "enforcing consequences" is so important, consider this:

Even as grown-ups, we are highly motivated by consequences:

- We pay our rent on time, **because** we don't want to incur a late fee.

- We get to the airport on time, **because** we don't want to miss our flight.

Again — by enforcing consequences when your child refuses to cooperate, you're helping them learn essential life lessons.

And while it may feel uncomfortable — especially when your child is screaming:

"You're so mean!"

or,

"You don't love me!"

Know that what you're doing is right ... and necessary.

WRITE YOUR PLAN:

In our home, we treat each other with care, **respect and love. Always.**

This means that we NEVER:

_____

_____

_____

And this means that we ALWAYS:

_____

_____

_____

In our home, we have certain rules. These rules are:

_____

_____

_____

These rules are important because ...

_____

_____

_____

When somebody breaks a rule, there is a consequence.

Here are the consequences for each rule:

_____

_____

_____

We have these rules — and we treat each other with care, respect and love — because we want to be the BEST family we can possibly be.

Signed:

_____
Parent

_____
Parent

Excellent!

Next:

You'll **learn how to hold a "family meeting".**

At the meeting, you'll share the new plan and secure your child's **respect and cooperation.**

STEP **7**

Share the Plan and Gain Cooperation.

Just like grown-ups, children want to understand WHY a particular request is being made.

They need a good, sensible reason.

Example:

"Don't pull the cat's tail, it might scratch you." ...

Or,

"You brush your teeth, so you won't get cavities."

This means:

"Because I said so" just doesn't cut it.

Your job — when you hold a family meeting — is to articulate, in an age-appropriate way, WHY things are going to be done differently from now on.

This script can help you do that.

FAMILY MEETING SCRIPT:

I asked you to be here today because there's something I want to talk about.

It's very important that you listen all the way until the end.

I'll let you know when it's time to add your thoughts.

Lately, I've been feeling frustrated about

_____

_____

_____

When

_____

_____

_____

happens, it is not acceptable.

And as your parent, it is my responsibility to make things right.

From now on, in our home, there are **some new rules** *and* **new consequences** *for not following those rules.*

I am setting these rules because **they will help you grow up to be the best person you can be.**

I am going to share them with you, now.

{read your entire plan — the new rules and consequences}

These new rules will create a much happier home for everyone.

I'm going to put them

_____

so you can see them every day.

Thank you for listening.

Do you have any questions?

A few tips to help your family meeting go smoothly:

— Make sure that you're calm and relaxed before you show up for the meeting.

(This might mean taking some deep breaths, or even doing the exercise in Step 1 of this Guide beforehand, in private).

— Acknowledge that YOU are the leader: the person responsible for setting rules and enforcing them.

Sometimes, you might need to start the meeting with an **apology**:

"I'm sorry. I have let you down.

Your tantrums and rudeness are not acceptable, and I've let you get away with it. That hasn't helped you.

I have not been the best parent, and for that, I'm sorry.

But that's going to change now, because I know what I need to do to teach you how to behave / gain your cooperation, and that's what I'm going to share with you at this meeting."

— As you set the rules, you can also brainstorm with your child to determine what the consequences will be for non-compliance.

Kids often come up with interesting consequences, and asking for their input helps them feel engaged and respected in this process.

— If your child is under the age of 10, it's a good idea to create some kind of chart to record good behavior with stickers or stars.

You and your child should spend a few moments reviewing the chart, every day, to **reinforce** the rules and **celebrate** good choices.

— Keep your comments and instructions brief and to the point.

Especially if you have young children attending the family meeting. Their attention-span is **short**.

Speak clearly, simply and concisely.

— Be sure to give a reason for every rule that you set.

— When it's your child's turn to ask questions, respond **patiently**.

— Have your child repeat back to you what each rule is and what the consequence will be for non-compliance

This way, you'll know they **understand**.

— When introducing a new rule, you can give your child a few warnings to get it right (the amount of warnings will depend on their age.

Younger kids (0-6) will need more warnings (say three or four) because their short-term memory is not as solid yet.

Generally, for children ages 7 and above, two warnings should be sufficient.

Tell your child ahead of time, at the family meeting, that they'll get **two warnings.**

And if they behave **inappropriately**, after that, a **consequence** will apply.

— It's critical to let children know ahead of time, what the consequence will be.

This way, you're encouraging them to **think** before they act ... and to **choose wisely.**

Example:

"If I don't brush my teeth, then no bedtime story."

or,

"If I violate curfew, I'll be grounded next weekend."

— Be careful about "asking" your child to do something. That allows a window for the child to say, "No."

Your child needs to feel your **authority**.

This means you need to **command compliance** by politely-but-firmly instructing your child on what to do.

A few tips to help your FOLLOW-UP meetings go smoothly:

After your first family meeting — where you lay out the new rules and consequences — it's a good idea to set up a couple of follow-up meetings to check in and make adjustments, as necessary.

At these follow-up meetings, you can ...

- **Review** your child's "chart."

- **Read** through the new rules and consequences, again.

- **Reiterate** the reasons for each rule, again.

If your child has back-slid a bit, you could say:

It's my job to make sure you understand the rules.

It's also my job to enforce the consequences we've discussed, when you don't follow the rules.

Now that we've gone over everything again, and you've repeated it all back to me, I know that you understand.

And I know you are going to do better.

STEP **8**

Celebrate Your Success!

There's a difference between "bribing" your child in the hopes of "winning" their cooperation, and **"celebrating"** with your child when things are going well.

As your child becomes more cooperative, take note. Call attention to their successes.

These little moments of encouragement will keep things moving in the right direction.

Try saying:

"The last time I asked you to

_____

_____

happened.

But this time,

_____

_____

_____

happened instead. I'm so proud of you!"

Or:

"Remember when you used to

_____

_____

_____?

Now, you're doing

_____

_____

_____

That's excellent!"

A few (cautionary) words on "celebration."

Be sure to celebrate success **only** if there has been **consistent** compliance for a reasonable period of time — usually at least two weeks.

If you're celebrating a behavior that your child is not yet consistently complying with, you could be giving your child a message that "less than" is "good enough."

Don't plan a "special" celebration unless your child has done something exceptional — beyond what is typically required.

— Perhaps your child put **extra effort** into a writing project for school, doing much more than was required, and the teacher was so impressed that she recommended the essay be published in the school magazine.

— Or perhaps your child woke up early to tidy up the entire living room, as a "surprise" for you — when that's not a chore they'd been assigned.

That would be cause for **a special celebration.**

Again: be careful not to set a precedent of having to do something for your kids — like buying a toy or a special dessert — every time they comply with a rule.

The best celebration is always a few words of **loving praise** — followed by a **hug**.

No additional rewards, required.

AFTER THE FAMILY MEETING (A FEW CLOSING WORDS):

Your child is depending on YOU to give them the BEST start in life.

And while parenting may feel like a challenge, at times, giving your child a good start isn't a "mystery."

It's really just about teaching right from wrong — so that your child understands how the world works and what is expected of them. And your child deserves that training NOW.

They shouldn't have to wait until they're all grown up to learn those kinds of lessons.

Waiting until adulthood will set them up for a very hard road.

So, begin NOW.

If you guide your child with **conviction and consistency**, your child is likely take your guidance seriously.

The results?

Noticeable.

At the same time ... **don't be hard on yourself** if you feel like:

— Things are moving too slowly.

or even,

— Dipping backwards at times.

Just focus on implementing firm, fair guidance with love.

By modeling that behavior consistently, it's practically inevitably that you will gain your child's cooperation.

Love always wins!

MORE TIPS, MORE TOOLS

5 FAQs From Moms and Dads About Tricky Parenting Situations

Ready for even more tips and tools to do the best job ever for your child? Read on for my general answers to some of the more typical, burning questions that parents have asked (summarized here, to maximize learning). And get your pencil and paper ready for more tips and tools along with self-help exercises and worksheets.)

Enjoy!

Question No. 1 — Rebellious Youth

Teaching Kids To Respect Rules

My son is 3, and I try to live as a respectful, law-abiding person. And that's what I teach my son.

But as a mom, I know there are so many young people breaking the law and rebelling.

Why are they like this, I don't understand? Is this how my son is going to turn out?

Response:

First, there's absolutely no doubt that you are on the right track by teaching your son to be socially responsible and to live honorably.

That said, the negative behavior that you are pointing out in the youth, doesn't just happened. It is **learned**... it is developed.

Why are they like this...? you ask.

Simply put, unfortunate as it is, there are many parents who do not teach their child positive behavior.

They do not raise their children with **positive discipline** which would offer them guidance and direction to make **positive choices.**

Nor do these parents give their children the **attention** that they need.

What happens next in this unfortunate situation?

Their children are likely to be vulnerable to being influenced by undesirable factors, like **peer pressure.**

A young child is so easily influenced. This is why it is crucial that anyone who has influence over a child — parents, relatives, trusted childcare providers, teachers, etc. — must be **knowledgeable about healthy behavior** and the **impact of their role-modeling** on children with whom they come into contact.

Follow-Up Question

I don't mean to be judgmental, but again, as a parent, I really want to know why are there so many youth gangs, violence amongst youth, body piercing and other, what seems to me, 'distorted' body expressions by teens — like having pink hair or wearing clothes that have vulgar language on them?

Response:

While every child and every family environment is unique, it's not uncommon, once again, for the behavior that you're asking about, to be a result of **poor parenting**.

There's a strong possibility that parents of these children:

— **Ignored** them

— Were **too busy** to spend time with them

— Were **too critical** of them

and / or

— Were i**gnorant of their needs for attention**

The result?

If the natural need that children have for positive attention is not satisfied, these children may try to behave in such a way that gets them noticed (You couldn't help but notice the pink hair, right?)

Much of the "distorted" behavior, as you describe it, can be interpreted as **a cry for attention**:

— *Pay attention to me.*

— *Admire me for what I am.*

— *Admire me for who I am.*

Generally speaking, children (and adults) who adopt this **attention-seeking type of behavior**, are also invariably **searching for an identity**.

It is also likely that they experience **anxiety** and **low self-esteem.**

Why?

Because if moms and dads are not positive roles models, and they don't parent in a constructive, healthy way, the development of positive traits such as confidence and high self-esteem tend to be inhibited.

What happens next?

These children tend to develop **insecurities**, and lack a sense of self-worth and self-esteem.

Unless this is addressed and resolved, these deficits are likely to **carry over into adulthood** and can manifest as **anxiety** and a sense of **inferiority**.

A fix?

This is a huge topic, and as with any challenge, "the fix" is rarely a one-size fits all.

That said, in general, there are **two basic elements** that parents must set in place when it comes to teaching children to develop into adults who are law-abiding and conform to social standards.

Parents must:

1. Prioritize showing interest in their child
2. Teach positive social habits.

What's a good way for parents show interest?

One way, is to ensure that their children, and the family as a whole, experience **quality family time.**

This means **undistracted sharing.**

Undistracted sharing means that during family interactions no one :

— Uses their devices (smartphones, tablets, etc.)

— Watches television

— Listens to the radio

— Reads

The **exception** would be if the family is sharing these activities together.

Example:

A parent is reading a bedtime story to a child.

The reason quality family time can be so effective?

— It tends to **seal, cement and bond** familial relationships.

— It also offers opportunities for positive socialization.

So if you're a working parent, it's a good idea to try to spend time with your child before work in the morning or after work until bedtime.

A few final thoughts on your excellent question, and then an exercise to tie all of this together.

From the moment your son was born, he was dependent on you for **guidance and direction**.

Your role as a parent was (and still is) to love and teach your son as best you knew (and currently know) how.

Hopefully, you were (and still are) shaping your newborn / developing child's behavior with **positive discipline** and exposing him to **healthy growth experiences.**

The reason this so important for all parents to hear?

Because **good parenting** generates **healthy behavior** in a child.

Likewise, if a **child behaves poorly**, that behavior is invariably a product of **poor parenting.**

So what does good parenting mean, really?

Parents who raise their children responsibly, teach them to :

- Be confident

- Have a sense of being a part of the family

- Respect society's rules.

The result?

When moms and dads parent with these types of values, their children invariably grow-up to be **well-adjusted adults** who feel good about themselves and their contribution to society.

Thank you again for your question.

I hope that, now that you've read my response, your mind is a little more at ease that if you consistently apply the positive parenting principles outlined in this book, you are giving your son the opportunity to live a life founded on **happiness, health and strength**, regardless of how his peers and other youth may behave.

That said, undoubtedly parenting can be challenging, and to do it right, parents need lots of **confidence**. This next exercise can help.

Visualization Exercise

Find a quiet, private space in your home where you can take 3 to 5 minutes of quiet, uninterrupted time.

Sit comfortably and close your eyes.

Take a deep breath in.

Exhale.

Repeat (inhale, exhale).

Now, imagine that your son is observing your positive role-modeling.

Picture your son happily adopting your positive traits.

Notice his caring and respectful qualities.

Notice the healthy pride he feels about following the rules.

Visualize yourself:

— Praising him for behaving so well.

— Telling him how much you love him, how much he means to you.

Observe the beautiful family bond that is growing between your and your son.

Spend a few moments confidently enjoying this visualization.

When you're ready, open your eyes… feeling confident and strong.

Question No. 2 — Chaotic Mornings

Providing Structure and Consistency for Your Children

Mornings in our household are chaotic and stressful.

My 7-year-old son and 9-year-old daughter typically dawdle, watch too much TV in the morning, and end up running late... and I turn into a nag (and sometimes "lose my cool" and yell) as I try to get them out the door on time and into the car so I can take them to school.

I'm always telling (lecturing?) them in the car, that they need to be on time, but it hasn't helped. They argue back a bit and try to make excuses. Sometimes it seems like they're listening what I'm saying. Still... nothing changes.

How can I get my kids (and me) on track in the mornings?

Response:

The experience that your children have in the mornings is so important. It sets the tone for their day, before they venture out into the world.

A few things that must be in place:

1. Establish Rules

To achieve your positive and necessary goal of making your children's morning experience **calm and nurturing,** instead of

chaotic, be sure to establish rules that clearly and simply, lay out for your children how you expect them to behave.

Some general things that your children may need to do the night before, include:

- Choosing their school clothes
- Packing their school bag

2. Develop Routines

Routines (repetitive sets of activities) are essential, especially on weekdays.

Children like routines for three primary reasons. Routines provide them with:

1. **Structure**
2. **Consistency**
3. **Predictability**

Example:

The morning routine would involve:

- Waking-up
- Getting dressed

- Eating breakfast
- Brushing teeth
- Getting school bag
- Being ready, on time, to leave for school

Other activities where routines should also be set up, include:

- Meals
- Homework
- Chores
- Bath
- Bedtime

Follow-Up Question

Those suggestions sound great I'd like to try them, but whenever I tell my kids about a new rule or a new routine that I want them to follow, they protest and tantrum — and they just won't stop. It's awful.

So to keep the peace, I give in and back off.

Then I feel like a failure as a parent, but at least I don't have to hear the tantrums any more!

I really want to try your ideas now, and usually I'm a good problem-solver, but when it comes to tantrums, I feel like I'm a weak parent.

Response:

Imagine, for a moment, that **mornings** in your household are **calm, nourishing and supportive** for your children (and also for you!) … and that **everything is flowing** just beautifully.

Here's an incredibly powerful tool to make this possible: it involves giving yourself a pep talk in writing.

You've probably heard the phrase, *"We're our own worst enemy"*, and perhaps that even applies to you.

Well, here's a chance to counter that perception by writing down a pep talk that you can take a look at whenever you need some **support or encouragement**.

Start Here, With This Writing Exercise To Get on Your Own Side.

It begins with identifying five positive qualities about yourself as a parent. Try not to over-think your answers or judge yourself if they sound "silly." **Self-criticism is never ok**.

Just write whatever comes to mind.

It's all good.

When it comes to being a parent:

One thing I really appreciate about myself is

_____

_____

_____

Another thing I'm pleased that I do is

_____

_____

_____

One thing that I feel is a real strength of mine is

_____

_____

_____

One thing I'm glad I'm teaching my children is

_____

_____

One strong quality of mine that I'm passing on to my children is

_____

_____

One area where I am going to improve is

_____

_____

_____

Generally, right now, I'm feeling

_____

_____

_____

What if nothing positive comes to mind?

Some parents to whom I've suggested this exercise, have responded by saying:

I can't think of any positive qualities.

My reply:

Try to think a little harder, or make some qualities up.

Here's usually happens next.

Their **creativity** starts to flow, and pretty soon they're writing a profile of themselves as **one heck of a parent!**

This written pep talk can be a great first step to being a **confident parent.** It can also bring you a lot closer to being able **calm the chaos** with a solid morning routine for your kids.

Remember: Read this pep talk whenever you need a boost of confidence.

Question No. 3 — Lenient Parenting

Using Positive Discipline To Promote Positive Choices

I was raised by strict parents who punished us. This was their way of making us do what they wanted.

It was a nightmare, so I've avoided disciplining my 7-year-old. I thought that was the right thing to do and that with love from me and his dad, and giving him whatever he wants, he'd feel loved and develop in a healthy way.

But now he rebels when he can't get his way. I don't know what to do. When I was growing up with strict parents, I vowed that if I ever had kids, I'd never treat them like that.. no punishment for my kids!

Response:

I'm sorry your childhood was so difficult.

Please know that **positive discipline** is **not punitive**. Discipline teaches children how to focus on goals, which in turn promotes self-discipline.

What is self-discipline?

It is essentially the ability to set a goal, and stick to it. It is self-direction.

Testing the limits

Since your child is **routinely** rebelling, his behavior is more than **rebelling to test limits**, which is a natural tendency that children display from **time to time.**

Consequences

Therefore, consequences are in order. These should be:

— **Age-appropriate**

— **Not excessive, but not lenient**

It's important to give your child a choice.

For example,

"If you choose not to do your chores, you will not be able to go and play with your neighbor friend until you do."

This encourages your child to **think** about which choice he will make, and whether or not he wants to incur a consequence.

Just like **discipline is not punitive** (it is firm, fair guidance, consistently applied with love), neither are consequences.

Consequences are intended to be an **incentive** to your child to motivate him **make a positive choice.**

Setting your parenting intention

Now that you have a clearer understanding of the difference between positive discipline and punishment, and now that you know that positive discipline is different to the "discipline-punishment' you experienced as a child, you can set your intention to implement positive discipline. You can **make a commitment** teach your child to make positive choices. Such a critical life skill.

Not quite sure where to begin?

Start Here: Fill in the Blanks in This Writing Exercise ...

I define being a "good parent" as

___

___

___

I define teaching my child to lead a "successful life" as

___

___

___

I define a "well-behaved child" as

___

___

___

Some of the life skills that I'd like to teach my child are

_____

_____

_____

I want my child to know that he can't always have his way because

_____

_____

_____

I want my child to know that choices have consequences because

_____

_____

_____

Growing up, I want my child to be self-disciplined so that he can

_____

_____

_____

Growing up, I want my child to realize that

_____

_____

_____

Ultimately, I want my child to grow up into the kind of person who

_____

_____

_____

Next? Achieving Your Intentions ...

Now that you've written down a few of your values and hopes for your child, let's look at **achieving** these intentions.

To do this, you might want to dig a little deeper and look at the goals you've set for your child in the form of **questions**.

Then write the **answers** to how you can achieve these goals.

Another Writing Exercise: More Blanks To Fill in ...

How can I be a "good parent" for my child?

_____

_____

_____

How am I going to teach my child to lead a "successful life"?

_____

_____

_____

How am I going to teach my child to be "well-behaved"?

_____

_____

_____

What life skills am I going to teach my child?

_____

_____

_____

How will I teach my child the value of not always having his way?

_____

_____

_____

How will I teach/show my child that choices have consequences?

_____

_____

_____

How will I teach my child the value of being self-disciplined?

_____

_____

_____

What's one thing I'll be sure my child realizes while growing up?

_____

_____

_____

What kind of person do I want my child to grow up to become?

_____

_____

_____

Expanding your list

Once you have completed this second writing exercise, expand your list to include at least **six simple, attainable goals**.

Be sure that you're writing these goals down because you really "want" to, not because you feel that you "should".

Otherwise you may find that it's **hard to stay motivated** when your drive is based on **have to's** or what's expected of you.

GOAL #1

_____

_____

_____

GOAL #2

_____

_____

_____

GOAL #3

_____
_____
_____

GOAL #4

_____
_____
_____

GOAL #5

_____
_____
_____

GOAL #6

_____
_____
_____

Success

Some parents also find it useful to express their goals as if they have already happened.

Examples:

— *My son is cooperating beautifully.*

— *I'm so proud of my son for making positive choices.*

— *Peace at home. At Last.*

Positive statements

Another helpful tip involves expressing your goals **positively**, rather than **negatively**.

Example:

My son is cooperating beautifully.

Instead of

My son no longer throws a tantrum when he doesn't get his way.

Or

I'm so proud of my son for making positive choices.

Instead of

My son is not rebelling anymore.

Or

Peace at home. At Last.

Instead of

My son is no longer being defiant and resistant.

Question No. 4 — Parental Anger

Curbing Frustration and Tempers

I adore my 6-year-old, but when he acts out or doesn't do what he's told, sometimes me and his dad get frustrated... and we lose our tempers and blow up at him.

But yelling at him makes things worse - he just rebels more and I worry that my explosions are making him feel bad.

I really want to get a handle on my flare-ups, but am I overreacting by worrying about the impact of these flare-ups on my son?

Response:

No. You are right to be concerned. Children do tend to be affected by being on the receiving end of their parents' anger.

How are they affected?

This will vary, depending on the nature of the parent's anger, as well as the child's age, personality and temperament.

General examples:

— Some children who are accustomed to being around a parent's angry voice and angry face may **resist discipline.**

They tend to copy their parents' behavior, and resist conforming. Instead, they display **aggressive reactions and have attitude.**

— Many also **lack confidence,** thinking:

I'm bad, Mom and Dad are always mad at me.

— Other children try to always **please their parents**, in an effort to dodge their parents' rage.

These children also tend to be **"on guard"** around their parents, never knowing when the angry outburst will be, but trying to protect themselves from it.

— Then there are other children who tend to **lie** so they won't get yelled at.

— There are also others who respond to irate parents with **indifference and joking** around in front of them.

Sadly, the laughter as expressed by these children is not genuine. It's a shield. A defensive cover to hide their **pain and shame.**

Although children's reactions to parental flare-ups vary, when it comes down to it, many feel **angry and ashamed.**

They're also at risk for thinking that:

I can't seem to do anything right.

Perhaps you're thinking:

OK, so how can I handle frustrating situations with my kids without losing my cool?

Short answer:

Handle your anger rationally, so you can model confident behavior.

You might be wondering:

OK, but is that really possible when I'm raging, and putting my child at risk for raging as well?

Ideally, parents who are overreacting and need to learn to manage their anger, would do well to seek other outlets for their frustration — a safe, private environment where they can vent.

Example:

Some parents find that they need to let off steam in private before they're able to then manage their anger in front of their children.

I've known of many parents, who, if their buttons are triggered by interacting with their kids, politely excuse themselves and head to:

— the garage to punch a punching bag and vent.

Or

— To a room where they have privacy, and can **pound a pillow with a knotted towel and yell and vent** without being heard. Sometimes they'll turn on the radio or television to muffle sound.

After "letting off some steam" privately, these parents invariably feel composed, and ready to respectfully deal with their child's misbehavior, without yelling, cursing or name-calling.

Question No. 6 — Crying To Get Attention

Unified Parenting Minimizes Acting-Out

When it's time for our 9-year-old to do her nightly chore (clean up after dinner), she has a crying fit. Honestly, she cries like a baby.

I get frustrated and yell at her.

My husband takes things even further — he threatens to spank her, although luckily he never does.

I'm against spanking and we fight about this in front of our child.

How can we turn this situation around? It's been this way for years.

Response:

Think about WHY your daughter is crying… what does she get out of doing this?

Crying is her way of **getting attention**.

She is also **emulating your frustration.**

This is a clear signal to you and her dad… that both of you need to:

- **Stop reacting**

and

- **Be unified as parents**

As for your daughter's crying outbursts, they should be **ignored**.

Why?

Because when your daughter **doesn't get any reaction** from you to her crying, this immature "acting out" is likely to **disappear**.

Follow-Up Question

That makes a lot of sense. Thank you. I will share your answer with my husband.

Another question... this time about our 14-year-old. When we give her a chore to do, like washing the car, she refuses to do it unless we pay her or increase her allowance.

"My friends get paid for doing stuff like this," she says. "I should get paid too!"

What can we, as parents, do? How do we get her to cooperate?

Response:

Regarding payment, absolutely not.

If you were to pay her, here's the message you'd be giving her:

You have no obligation to do this chore, unless ...

You want the money.

But that is <u>not</u> teaching her anything about:

— Her **obligation** as a member of your family.

Or

— Being a **responsible** member of your family.

Instead, it's important to tell her:

You are part of this family, which means that you must help out.

As for her demand that you increase her allowance to compensate her for doing her chore, **an allowance has nothing to do with chores**.

An allowance consists of funds allocated for **personal spending.**

Example:

Buying gifts for family or friends on special occasions, like birthdays.

An allowance also helps children **learn to manage money.**

An allowance is **not** intended to be used **to persuade or bribe** children to do their chores.

In addition, if children do not do their chores, an allowance should **not** be withdrawn as a consequence.

Second Follow-Up Question

We also have a 15-year-old who doesn't respect us. Not only that, it's like she rules the house.

This next part is embarrassing, but... if she doesn't get her way, she pouts and complains and says she's going to run away. (I don't think that she actually means it, but she knows that her threat "gets to" me and her dad.) She is smart and does well in school.

We try to be firm with her, but we end up giving in. We've spoiled her and she'll only do her chores if we pay her.

She doesn't think she's spoiled, especially, "Compared to my friends who live the same way as I do."

How can we teach her to cooperate?

Response:

At her age, she's probably pretty set in her basic habits. This means that the window of opportunity for you, as a parent, to impact her behavior is smaller than it was, say 10 years ago.

That said, it's critical that you set a standard at home that prepares your daughter to **deal with life...** to cope with its demands.

You are not helping her by catering to her.

Why?

Because, she'll have a hard time coping when she goes out into the world and finds that there is a different standard to what she's used to.

Equip Your Child for the Real World

It's one thing to give in to your child at home, to avoid a battle and keep the peace. It's quite another thing for your child to find out that the real world doesn't work that way — that life doesn't "give in to us to appease us" and that benefits need to be earned.

Have the courage to teach your child to develop into a responsible, contributing person. Nourish your child's potential to live a successful life.

These parenting affirmations can keep things moving in a positive direction.

Try saying:

I remember when my 9-year-old used to

_____

_____

_____

When she had a chore to do.

Now, she's doing

_____

Because I **ignored her crying.** I'm proud of her.

The last time my 15-year-old had a chore to do

happened.

But this time,

happened instead. Because I **wouldn't pay her**. I'm proud of her.

WHAT'S NEXT?

RESOURCES... TO KEEP RAISING THE PARENTING BAR

I hope this Life Guide has been helpful. It is "technically" finished, but I wanted to give you some **more resources** on being **the BEST parent you can be** and **Being the BEST version of yourself**... in case you'd like to keep raising the parenting bar.

Here are some of my favorites— articles and books I authored,[1] other Life Guides I created, and inspiring insights I shared when I was interviewed by a reporter from the Weekend Today Show.

This is a no pressure zone... so savor at your leisure, and enjoy!

---

[1] All articles referenced in this section were published online.

HOW TO BE THE BEST PARENT YOU CAN BE

It Starts With You. How To Raise Happy, Successful Children By Being The Best Role Model You Can Possibly Be — A Guidebook, by Dr. Gelb

https://www.amazon.com/Starts-You-Successful-Becoming-Guidebook/dp/0692647392/ref=tmm_pap_swatch_0?_encoding=UTF8&qid=1553581148&sr=1-4

The Life Guide On How To Get Ready To Be A Parent — And Be The Best Mom Or Dad You Can Possibly Be.

http://drsuzannegelb.com/life-guide-get-ready-to-be-a-parent/

The Life Guide On Helping Your Teen Make Healthy Choices About Dating and Sex

http://drsuzannegelb.com/helping-teen-make-healthy-choices-dating-sex/

Praise for Dr. Gelb's Life Guides

"Dr. Gelb has a gentle spirit that instantly makes you feel like you've come home. The depth of her wisdom is undeniable, her curiosity is insatiable and her love is palpable. These qualities make her the perfect guide for life. In the pages of the Life Guides you will find practical and proven processes to support you in living your great life. Whether it's heart-centered wisdom on navigating the dating world, love-based strategies for becoming a parent, or reaching your ideal weight through kindness, Dr. Gelb's Life Guides are gifts to be treasured."

— Dr. Gemma Stone, Psychologist, Mentor, Author

Three Lessons You Must Teach Your Kids. (The sooner the better. But it's never too late)
— Published on my column "All Grown Up" on Psychology Today

https://www.psychologytoday.com/us/blog/all-grown/201503/parents-three-lessons-you-must-teach-your-kids

Why "Bribing" Your Child With Treats... Doesn't Work. And What Does
— Published on my column "All Grown Up" on Psychology Today

https://www.psychologytoday.com/blog/all-grown/201510/why-bribing-your-child-treats-doesn-t-work

Raising Kids Who Love Reading and Devour Books Voraciously
— Published on my column "All Grown Up" on Psychology Today

https://www.psychologytoday.com/us/blog/all-grown/201507/raising-kids-who-love-reading-devour-books-voraciously

"Mommy, Do You Love Your Blog More Than Me?" What To Do if Your Child Feels in Competition With Your Work
— Published on The Huffington Post

https://www.huffpost.com/entry/mommy-do-you-love-your-blog-more-than-me-what-to_b_58dde22ce4b0fa4c095987f2

3 Ways to Stop Your Teen From Making Risky Choices
— Published on The Huffington Post

http://www.huffingtonpost.com/dr-suzanne-gelb/3-ways-to-stop-your-teen-from-making-risky-choices-about-dating-and-sex_b_5925602.html

Good Parenting Isn't Complicated — Here's Why
—Originally Published on Maria Shriver; soon to be published on my column "All Grown Up" on Psychology Today

bit.ly/1QlQQsE

7 Dangerous Lessons We Need To Stop Teaching Our Kids
— Published on Mind Body Green

https://www.mindbodygreen.com/0-14586/7-dangerous-lessons-we-need-to-stop-teaching-our-kids.html

Spring Cleaning for Your Life [Part 1/3]
— Published on The Huffington Post

https://www.huffpost.com/entry/spring-cleaning-for-your_n_7253908

Time-Out. Getting the Most Out of This Popular Discipline Tactic
— Published in Family Advocate, Vol. 30, No. 1 (Summer 2007) American Bar Association

https://bit.ly/2FdxXYy

When the Other Parent Doesn't Play Fair
— Published in Family Advocate, Vol. 30, No. 1 (Summer 2007) American Bar Association

bit.ly/1QmYYpq

Raising an Organized Child In a Blended Family
— Published in Family Advocate, Vol. 36, No. 1 (Summer 2013) American Bar Association

https://bit.ly/2HJgxFW

HOW TO BE THE BEST VERSION OF YOURSELF

6 Self-Sabotaging Habits You Need To Drop Right Now
— Published on Mind Body Green.

https://www.mindbodygreen.com/0-14014/6-selfsabotaging-habits-you-need-to-drop-right-now.html

The Life Guide on How To Reach Your Ideal Weight — Through Kindness Not Craziness,

http://drsuzannegelb.com/life-guide-ideal-weight/

Praise for Dr. Gelb's Life Guides

"Learning how to love yourself and treat yourself kindly — even when your life, career, body, and relationships aren't 'totally perfect' — is one of the hardest things to do. Dr. Suzanne Gelb breaks down the art of self-love into practical steps. No woo-woo vagueness. Just easy-to-follow exercises pulled from her 28-year

career in the field. If you're looking for practicality and effectiveness, these Life Guides are a steal of a deal."

—Susan Hyatt, Master Certified Life Coach, Published Author

"This Life Guide came at the perfect time. My two fears about losing weight were dispelled immediately and it was such a relief to know that I can start looking after myself without the worry of going to the gym or going on another desperate diet.

The audio helped re-frame the reasons why I've let my weight spiral out of control and the work book helped me set out an action plan. Thanks, Dr. Gelb, for your Life Guide, here's to a happier, healthier life."

—Amanda Herbert, photographer

If You Want to Make Tomorrow Less Stressful—Start Tonight
— Published on The Muse

You can find this article on my column on the Muse. The column is called, "Be Well At Work."

https://www.themuse.com/advice/if-you-want-to-make-tomorrow-less-stressfulstart-tonight

Side note: The Muse is an award-winning online career resource, with over 4 million quality, professional members. I'm honored to have received the praise below, from Adrian Granzella Larssen, Editor-in-Chief, in response to an article that I wrote for The Muse:

"Wow! This is fantastic stuff. You're clearly incredible at what you do, and I'm so thrilled to share your advice with our audience!"

You Are The Best Investment You'll Ever Make
— Published on my column, "All Grown Up," on Psychology Today.

https://www.psychologytoday.com/blog/all-grown/201511/you-are-the-best-investment-youll-ever-make

3 Ways to Get What You Need From Terrible Communicators.
— Published on TIME; originally published on my column "Be Well At Work" on The Muse

http://time.com/3768073/3-ways-get-from-terrible-communicators/

Why Positive Affirmations Don't Always Work (And What Does)
— Published on Tiny Buddah;

http://tinybuddha.com/blog/why-positive-affirmations-dont-always-work-and-what-does/

How to Succeed Everywhere: 10 Tips for Balance at Work, Home, in Relationships
— Written by Shelby Marra, published online on NBC's Today.

https://www.today.com/health/how-become-high-achieving-woman-work-your-relationship-parent-t33071

Side note: As my colleague, friend, and gifted writing teacher, Alex Franzen said: *"THIS IS AMAZING! Being interviewed by a reporter from NBC's Today Show? Uh, that's the big leagues!"*

Yes, that's what happened. Shelby Marra with NBC's Today Show in New York, requested an interview with me so that she could write this article featuring me, for TODAY.com's Successful Women series.

How Successful People Do More in 24 Hours Than the Rest of Us Do in a Week
— Published on Newsweek; also published on my column, "Be Well At Work," on The Muse

https://www.newsweek.com/career/how-successful-people-do-more-24-hours-rest-us-do-week

The Love Tune-Up: How to Amp Up the Love That's Naturally Inside You to Enjoy Happy, Healthy Relationships.

https://amzn.to/2UzTSP6

ABOUT THE AUTHOR

Dr. Suzanne Gelb, Ph.D., J.D. is a psychologist, life coach, TV commentator and author.

Dr. Gelb's inspiring insights on personal growth have been featured on more than 200 radio programs, 260 TV interviews, and online on Time, Newsweek, Forbes, The Huffington Post, NBC's Today, Psychology Today, Positively Positive, The Muse and many other places, as well.

Dr. Gelb served as a parenting expert writer for Hawaii Parent magazine for over 14 years and appeared regularly on television to share tips on a parenting segment for 6 years.

As a contributing writer to the Psychology Today, where she has a regular column, "All Grown Up," Dr. Gelb has written articles on parenting, including, **10 Vital Life Lessons to Teach Your Kids Before They Turn 10**, and **10 Ways to Become the Parent Your Children Really Need**. Her powerful article, **7 Dangerous Lessons We Need To Stop Teaching Our Kids,** was published on Mind Body Green.

Dr. Gelb believes that it is never too late to become the person — and parent — you want to be. Strong. Confident. Calm. Creative. Free of all of the burdens that have held you back — no matter what has happened in the past.

To learn more, visit DrSuzanneGelb.com.

OTHER BOOKS BY THE AUTHOR

It Starts With You – How to Raise Happy, Successful Children by Becoming the Best Role-Model You Can Possibly Be. A Guidebook For Parents.

Helping Your Teen Make Healthy Choices About Dating and Sex. (A Life Guide.)

How to Get Ready to Be a Parent and Be the Best Mom or Dad You Can Possibly Be. (A Life Guide.)

How to Forgive the One Who Hurt You Most. (A Life Guide.)

How to Deal With People Who Drive You Absolutely Nuts. (A Life Guide.)

Aging With Grace, Strength and Self-Love. (A Life Guide.)

How to Navigate Being Single and Savor Your Dating Adventure. (A Life Guide.)

The Love Tune-Up: How to Amp Up the Love That's Naturally Inside You to Enjoy Happy, Healthy Relationships.

How to Rekindle That Spark and Create the Relationship and Sex Life That You Want. (A Life Guide.)

How to Find Work That You Love When You're Stuck in a Job That You Hate. (A Life Guide.)

How to Reach Your Ideal Weight Through Kindness, Not Craziness. (A Life Guide.)

Welcome Home: Release Addiction and Return to Love.

How to Care for Yourself When You're a Caregiver for Somebody Else. (A Life Guide.)

Real Men Don't Vacuum. And Other Misguided Myths That Cause Conflict in Relationships.

INDEX[2]

A

accountability, 2
age-appropriate, 50, 73
angry, 6, 7, 87, 88
attention, 18, 53, 56, 62, 63, 64, 102
authoritarian, 17

B

bad, 3, 13, 23, 33, 44, 87, 88
behave well, 2
bribes, 23, 24
bribing, 12, 23, 56, 98
broken, 3

C

change, 1, 3, 17, 19, 21, 27, 36, 37, 52
change your child's behavior, 1
change your parenting, 1

confidence, 2, 5, 30, 64, 67, 75, 88
consequence, 13, 21, 25, 47, 53, 54, 77, 95
consistency, 1, 59, 69, 70
consistent, 13, 22, 43, 58
conversations, 5
cooperate, 1, 3, 4, 6, 18, 21, 22, 24, 29, 31, 42, 45, 91, 93
cooperation, 1, 2, 4, 5, 21, 28, 31, 33, 48, 49, 52, 56, 60
creativity, 75
crying, 90, 91, 95

D

defiance, 28
dilemma, 1
disobeying, 9
disorganization, 32
do what's right, 2
drama, 2

---

[2] The page numbers in this index refer to the printed version of this book. If you click on the link provided, you will reach the beginning of that print page. If necessary, scroll forward from that page to locate the corresponding page on your e-reader.

E

exhausted, 3

F

FAQs, 61
fill-in-the-blank, 5
fill-in-the-blank worksheets, 5, 37, 78
frustrated, 3, 18, 24, 29, 31, 50, 87, 90

G

guidance, 2, 22, 59, 60, 62, 66, 77
guilty, 12, 13

H

harsh, 25, 31
healing, 36
healthy respect for authority, 2

J

journal, 18

L

leaders, 4

leadership, 4
lenient, 15, 25, 76, 77
listen, 3, 50
listening, 6, 51, 69

M

make a plan, 43
manipulate, 14. 23, 24, 30
manipulation, 21, 24
misbehave, 17
misbehavior, 3, 89

N

nag, 25, 26, 69
nagging, 3, 26

O

organized, 26, 32, 100

P

parenting, 1, 2, 15, 16, 17, 18, 21, 31, 34, 35, 43, 59, 61, 63, 67, 76, 77, 90, 94, 96, 99, 104
parenting skills, 2
partner, 6, 13
patterns, 11, 12, 14, 15, 18, 19, 34, 35, 36, 37, 43

peace at home, 2, 85, 86
privacy, 7, 89
private, 7, 52, 68, 89
problem, 9, 17, 21
problems, 4, 17
punishment, 17, 76, 77, 78
punitive, 76, 77

R

reacting, 90
rebel, 17, 25, 31
rebelling, 62, 77, 86
resist, 27, 87
resources, 96
respect, 1, 2, 4, 5, 32, 42, 46, 47, 48, 62, 67, 93
responsibility, 2, 23, 26, 32, 51
role-modeling, 63, 68
rules, 1, 13, 17, 24, 28, 30, 40, 43, 46, 47, 51, 52, 53, 55, 62, 67, 68, 69, 70, 93

S

scripts, 5
security, 4
self-criticism, 72
self-esteem, 2, 64
self-worth, 24, 64
sensible, 49
solution, 1
stressful, 69, 101
support, 25, 72, 97

T

tantrums, 2, 23, 52, 71, 72
teenager, 3
tempers, 87
threatening, 12, 23
throwing a fit, 9
tips, 52, 55, 61, 102, 104
tired, 3, 21, 33
toddler, 3
tools, 61
trust, 5, 21, 42

U

understanding, 15, 20, 31, 77
unruly, 3, 9

V

vent, 7, 89
visualization exercise, 68

W

worksheets, 5, 61
worry, 87, 101

Y

yell, 7, 15, 69, 89, 90
yelling, 3, 15, 23, 32, 33, 87, 89

www.ingramcontent.com/pod-product-compliance
Lightning Source LLC
Chambersburg PA
CBHW020143130526
44591CB00030B/184